CATHERINE COOKSON WAS BORN IN TYNE DOCK, THE illegitimate daughter of a poverty-stricken woman, Kate, whom she believed to be her older sister. She began work in service but eventually moved south to Hastings, where she met and married Tom Cookson, a local grammar-school master. At the age of forty she began writing about the lives of the working-class people with whom she had grown up, using the place of her birth as the background to many of her novels.

Although originally acclaimed as a regional writer – her novel *The Round Tower* won the Winifred Holtby award for the best regional novel of 1968 – her readership soon began to spread throughout the world. Her novels have been translated into more than a dozen languages and more than 50,000,000 copies of her books have been sold in Corgi alone. Many of her novels have been made into successful television dramas, and more are planned.

Catherine Cookson's many bestselling novels established her as one of the most popular of contemporary women novelists. After receiving an OBE in 1985, Catherine Cookson was created a Dame of the British Empire in 1993. She was appointed an Honorary Fellow of St Hilda's College, Oxford in 1997. For many years she lived near Newcastle-upon-Tyne. She died shortly before her ninety-second birthday in June 1998 having completed 104 works, nine of which are being published posthumously.

BOOKS BY CATHERINE COOKSON

NOVELS

Kate Hannigan
The Fifteen Streets
Colour Blind
Maggie Rowan
Rooney
The Menagerie
Slinky Jane
Fanny McBride
Fenwick Houses
Heritage of Folly
The Garment
The Fen Tiger
The Blind Miller
House of Men
Hannah Massey
The Long Corridor
The Unbaited Trap
Katie Mulholland
The Round Tower
The Nice Bloke
The Glass Virgin
The Invitation
The Dwelling Place
Feathers in the Fire
Pure as the Lily
The Mallen Streak
The Mallen Girl

The Mallen Litter
The Invisible Cord
The Gambling Man
The Tide of Life
The Slow Awakening
The Iron Façade
The Girl
The Cinder Path
Miss Martha Mary Crawford
The Man Who Cried
Tilly Trotter
Tilly Trotter Wed
Tilly Trotter Widowed
The Whip
Hamilton
The Black Velvet Gown
Goodbye Hamilton
A Dinner of Herbs
Harold
The Moth
Bill Bailey
The Parson's Daughter
Bill Bailey's Lot
The Cultured Handmaiden
Bill Bailey's Daughter
The Harrogate Secret
The Black Candle

The Wingless Bird
The Gillyvors
My Beloved Son
The Rag Nymph
The House of Women
The Maltese Angel
The Year of the Virgins
The Golden Straw
Justice is a Woman
The Tinker's Girl
A Ruthless Need
The Obsession
The Upstart
The Branded Man
The Bonny Dawn
The Bondage of Love
The Desert Crop
The Lady on My Left
The Solace of Sin
Riley
The Blind Years
The Thursday Friend
A House Divided
Kate Hannigan's Girl
Rosie of the River
The Silent Lady

THE MARY ANN STORIES

A Grand Man
The Lord and Mary Ann
The Devil and Mary Ann

Love and Mary Ann
Life and Mary Ann
Marriage and Mary Ann

Mary Ann's Angels
Mary Ann and Bill

FOR CHILDREN

Matty Doolin
Joe and the Gladiator
The Nipper
Rory's Fortune

Our John Willie
Mrs Flannagan's Trumpet
Go Tell It To Mrs Golightly
Lanky Jones

Nancy Nutall and the
  Mongrel
Bill and the Mary Ann
  Shaughnessy

AUTOBIOGRAPHY

Our Kate
Catherine Cookson Country

Just a Saying
Let Me Make Myself Plain

Plainer Still

SHORT STORIES
The Simple Soul and other stories

JUST A SAYING

A FINAL PERSONAL ANTHOLOGY

CATHERINE COOKSON

CORGI BOOKS

JUST A SAYING
A CORGI BOOK: 0 552 14815 6

Originally published in Great Britain by Bantam Press,
a division of Transworld Publishers

PRINTING HISTORY
Bantam Press edition published 2002
Corgi edition published 2003

5 7 9 10 8 6 4

Set in 11.5 on 13pt Granjon.

Corgi Books are published by Transworld Publishers,
61-63 Uxbridge Road, London W5 5SA,
a division of The Random House Group Ltd,
in Australia by Random House Australia (Pty) Ltd,
20 Alfred Street, Milsons Point, Sydney, NSW 2061, Australia,
in New Zealand by Random House New Zealand Ltd,
18 Poland Road, Glenfield, Auckland 10, New Zealand
and in South Africa by Random House (Pty) Ltd,
Endulini, 5a Jubilee Road, Parktown 2193, South Africa.

Printed and bound in Great Britain by
Cox & Wyman Ltd, Reading, Berkshire.

Papers used by Transworld Publishers are natural, recyclable products made
from wood grown in sustainable forests. The manufacturing processes
conform to the environmental regulations of the country of origin.

CONTENTS

Introduction / *9*

PART ONE: NONE SO BLIND
None So Blind / *13*
The Wonder of It / *17*
But the Beginning / *19*
The Dark Side of Us / *21*
The Summer of '69 / *22*
Autumn / *24*
Without Winter / *25*
I Am Missing Something / *26*
When I Die / *28*
Imagination / *29*
Eeh! Poetry / *30*
Hot Summer / *32*
The Sky / *35*
The Northerner / *36*
The Return / *37*
The Joy of the Country / *38*
Understanding / *39*
Today / *41*
From My Bed / *42*
Silence / *43*

PART TWO: THE DAILY ROUND

Slow Me Down / 47

Just a Saying / 48

Youth / 50

I Am Young / 51

Laugh Gentle / 52

Washday 1912 / 53

The Workers / 54

The Test / 55

The Daily Round / 56

The Dragging Chain / 59

Tired / 60

Breakdown / 61

Death / 63

New Epilogue / 64

Wants / 65

Loss / 66

Old Age / 67

Night / 68

Me / 69

17 March 1970 / 71

Retirement / 72

So Easy to Read / 75

Age / 76

Auto-suggestion / 77

Atmosphere / 78

PART THREE: MY HEART IS YOU

Another Kind of Love / *81*

To All Bairns / *82*

Protect Me / *84*

The Lonely One / *85*

Once Known / *86*

Going Bust / *89*

Bottle Blonde / *90*

Do Not Tempt Me / *91*

Bitches / *93*

Hello, Kitty Dear! / *97*

Who's to Blame Him / *98*

On Your Wedding Day / *99*

Opinions / *101*

Partners / *103*

A Wife? / *105*

Sisters All / *106*

Brushed Nylon / *109*

The Loser / *110*

Distant Friends / *111*

The Individual / *113*

A Son / *114*

Me Granny / *115*

The Virgin / *116*

What Is a Wife? / *118*

Marriage – True Love / *120*

My Heart Is You / *122*

Index of First Lines / *123*

INTRODUCTION

CATHERINE COOKSON USED POETRY AS A MEANS OF communication in the same way as she used words to illuminate the magical stories she wrote; and she was also a painter who could illustrate her thoughts and feelings with considerable skill. The illustrations in *Let Me Make Myself Plain* (Bantam Press, 1988) make this very clear.

Catherine's poems say exactly what she felt at the time of writing, and, as always with her work, she believed in clarity of expression and colourful imagery – not for her the obscure or veiled comment. She was self-taught in the art of writing, and used to say that of all the thousands of letters she received she was most proud of those from schoolteachers who praised her use of the English language and said how much it encouraged their pupils. As Charles Spencer wrote in the *Sunday Telegraph* about *The Tinker's Girl*: 'Cookson writes plain English of considerable power . . . the characters are drawn with a mixture of strength and subtlety.'

Always direct, Catherine hated pomposity and she had no 'side' or feeling of self-importance. She would talk to anyone and everyone – preferably on the telephone in her later years – and her concern for others was legendary. The telephone was her lifeline, and words in poetry and prose her life.

Catherine's poetry was always definite, and how she hated the word 'nice'. As she makes clear in the opening to *Plainer Still* (Bantam Press, 1995), she wants a positive reaction, not a lukewarm euphemism. She wrote poems all her life, certainly from the age of nineteen, long before she started writing her wonderful novels. She covered every subject under the sun with clarity, with feeling and with understanding.

As she always liked having the last word, here is how Catherine herself described her poetry (in *Let Me Make Myself Plain*, p. 9):

I am known as a writer of novels, but my husband, bless him, has always maintained that I am a poet. However, my idea of a true poet is derived from the writings of men such as Donne, Wordsworth, Byron, Shelley, Keats, and in modern times, Betjeman, and each of these is understandable to the ordinary person, except perhaps Donne, who needs some probing. At the same time I also hold that writers such as the often ridiculed Ella Wheeler Wilcox were genuine poets; she, in particular, could transmit homespun philosophy. Like Kipling, she was a poet for the people.

Still, what does this leave me? Not a poet; oh no, because what I put down in this form of writing has neither true rhyme nor rhythm. It is merely, to my mind, Prose On Short Lines.

PART ONE

NONE SO BLIND

None So Blind

I am not blind,
Yet up till now
I have never seen
The abundant wonders
Strewn before my eyes.
I look down on the earth
On which I stand:
The grass is green
On top of black soil,
Spoil of myriad trees;
Below is rock,
Tear-stained in strata
From forgotten aeons;
To my right
A dip,
No! a fissure,
No! a gorge,
Bitten out by the might
Of torrents, glacier-born
On some far continent.
The agony of their birth
A peal,
Not of bells
But of hells,
Created by ice-crushing sound
Before human ear had yet been born
To hear

Crescendo
That would have split the sense,
Never more to hear.
Yet I stand
Now in wonder
To ask,
Why has it taken so long
To awaken this sleeping sense?
Or is it,
I have been aware
The wonder was there;
But, as Davies said,
I took no time
'To stand and stare'.
Only now, the end approaching fast,
My eyes open wide,
I see at last;
But eighty years
Is long to wait
This ecstatic moment
In which I contemplate
In wonder swamped
The past
And the instinct to create.
Who is to blame?
Fate?
Though what is fate

But the weave of life
Threaded with free will,
Which again is the gift of God,
So they tell.
And do not forget
He also promised hell.
But that was after death.
Can God have gone astray?
For to suffering women
It is here today,
And to stay
Their whole life long.
Something's wrong.

Face to face, baring my spiritual warts,
I deny the faith
While accepting the spirit
Which they term God;
I rant against hypocrisy
And cant
While applauding
My own version of truth,
Which I put over
With ruthless sincerity,
Hoping it will convert,
While I say,
Let everyone be free

To choose their own road.
So unlike the toad,
Ugly and venomous,
I wear no precious jewel in my head,
Only a mass of contradictions
Instead.

The Wonder of It

Look! I am alive,
My hand is using my pen.
Look! I am alive,
My eyes are seeking all men,
Mankind;
And them not alone,
But trees and flowers and water.
By the wonder of the sun
I see this whole day.
And I can speak my praise aloud,
I am not mute.
I can hear it,
I am not deaf.
I am alive.
To prove it . . . look! I walk.
Hear me! I am alive,
I can walk, talk,
See and hear,
So why waste time on the end,
And the fear
Of no longer being aware,
For in this minute
I am alive.
Isn't that enough?
What could be more clear?
Isn't this moment worth
The longings of all the dead

Who have cried,
Give us this day
Our daily bread?
For they no longer are being fed,
They're dead.
But I am alive.
I am alive.
So give thanks to the gods
For the appreciation of the gift,
Understood in this second of time
And transmuted
In my feeble rhyme,
For there may not be
Another time.

But the Beginning

A bare patch of ground became a
    beautiful scene,
With lawns and flowers and evergreen;
And so still at times did it seem
I couldn't but think that God had been,
Had been at dawn and stood and gazed
At the scene of our labour and sweat,
And said, This is but the beginning,
I have greater beauties stored for you yet.
I give to those who work the secret of the soil,
The bursting bud, the straining stem,
    the spreading bough and bark,
And tempt their appetite to earth and their
    ear to the lark.

I began my autobiography with these lines in 1956. They expressed my feelings at that time, but during the twelve years it took me to complete my life story the bitterness ebbed somewhat, and I replaced them with 'To All Bairns'. Yet these lines still remain true...

The Dark Side of Us

From the seed all sorrow,
All rage,
All pain,
All malice,
Greed,
All ill-gotten gain,
All spite,
Revenge
And lust,
From that grain,
Begat
Through habit, love
Or urge,
All that deals death
To body and mind
And would strangle,
As if with a rope,
Except it holds
In its fibre
A purge . . .
Called hope.

The Summer of '69

Remember the summer of '69?
It went right through autumn
And touched on winter,
When the days were short
But still fine,
In that summer of '69.

The fogs came
But did not stay;
The sun shone every day
Until a slight weariness
Crept in.
The wonderful sun
Became a bane:
Guiltily you longed for rain,
For a dull day
Of drizzle and fret;
Yet you cooed with the crowd
When the day was fine
In that wonderful summer of '69.

And the lesson one learnt
When weariness crept in
Was that seasons, like men,
Should know when to stop
As well as begin,
For you can have too,
Too much of any good thing.

Autumn

Brittle leaves gold and brown,
Zigzagging, floating, fluttering down:
Chestnut burrs strewn around,
Acorns popping, arresting sound;
The sun in mist, sailing o'er
Wooded hillsides of fairy lore,
A fluted note, quiet, rare,
Vibrating softly the clear air;
Hills red with dying fern,
Cold clearer water in the burn;
Patterns of light and shade,
Of such to me is autumn made.

On such a day as this, soft and warm,
Fragrant with autumn smells and
     fresh-turned loam,
And birdsong, not shrill but softly sweet;
With nature's gold-brown carpet for
     your feet,
The air folding you like a gossamer veil,
No stir, no quiver to ruffle a sail.
On such a day as this ... to live, who
     could fail?

Without Winter

Without winter, what would spring do?
It couldn't bring out fresh green grass
Or sweep the streams clean
Or give rest to the trees, great and small,
Or paint their leaves in beauty
Ready for their fall to carpet the way;
Without winter there'd be no short day
Giving long night to rest;
Without winter, spring at its best
Would be just another day;
So, without sorrow could we appreciate joy?
Yes, but its constancy would cloy:
The pattern of nature is set for us to follow
Even when it takes us into winter's sorrow.

I Am Missing Something

The pall of Christmas hangs again:
No looking forward to the crib,
Not even to the pocket-striven Christmas fair.
Nowhere in it do I glimpse wonder.
My heart is bare of childhood wrappings;
Whisky or beer cannot lighten the road to cheer.
I have a need, a craving to recapture something.
But what?
Could I strip myself of years
And drop into childhood space,
Would that explain my case
To the God who was born a boy?
Would he then inject me with joy?
And cure my complaint called life?
. . . But no.
He cannot go against his staff,
Who are holding payment until I die,
But who have promised, in his name,
A percentage good and high.

I go on strike against such theory.
Anyway I cannot believe in the God-man
If I don't believe in the boy.
But this strike brings no pay
And I long for food, for I am starved
     spiritually today.

Reach out, childhood, and draw me back
     down the years;
Nothing is impossible.
Let me view once again the crib with tears.

When I Die

When I die
Let me lie
For a time in my bed.
My body may be dead,
But my spirit is alive
Not ready yet for transit
To the other side.
Time enough when one is ready
To let go,
When one will know
The short journey out
Will be tomorrow or so.

So take comfort, heart of mine,
Our spirits cannot be parted,
For each is a part of the divine.

Imagination

The windows are clean
That she looks through,
With brown-crowned trees
Dusting skies of blue,
And birds like arrows
Before her sight
Dart into an immensity of light;
Fragile and wax-like,
The roses seem
Untouchable, like beauty
In a dream;
Whence come chrysanthemums
With frosty elegance,
Against whose beauty
She has no defence;
She sees all these
Through her windows bright,
Sees them there
Both day and night;
Don't say she looks
On a back-yard small,
A paved path, a stone wall,
Where of beauty
There is nothing at all.

Eeh! Poetry

What rhymes with cat?
Mat, rat, sat, fat.
But you've no need
To worry any more
On that score.
And metre?
Da-di-di, da-da.
It stops you thinking.
You won't get far,
Every thought checked
By da-di-da.
No,
Just put down everything
That comes into your head:
When at work,
Lying abed,
On a bus,
And thus,
Like me,
You will write
And fight
Your problems
On to paper;

And so freely
Your thoughts will flow;
But for God's sake, Joe,
Don't you go
And call our prattlings
Poetry!

Hot Summer

The meadow, sheep-cropped to earth's grey;
The wagon, high piled with brittle
    sun-bleached hay;
The horse, body steaming, knows it pulls the
    last load of the day;
And workers, faces streaked with labour sweat,
Know for them the day is not done yet.

In the bramble hedge the birds are still,
Feathers brushed in the warm green tangle;
A blackbird drops to the path
And spreads wide its wings to take a sunbath;
A foolish rabbit eases from the bakehouse
    of its burrow,
And a falcon, wings spread blotting out the sun
To the hypnotized eye,
Knows it need hunt no more until the morrow.

The river runs slow,
Revealing boulders which view the sky
Whose refraction only has flicked them
    for a century or so,
And fish pant their last without a hook,
And the otter, lying barely wet, strains to recall
The deafening roar of the river's bass chords;
And I, lying under a tree,
Attempt to capture it all in words.

Taking a break from my desk, I went to the study window and looked up into the sky, and as I did so I realized that one rarely looks up into the sky, especially in a town.

I am surrounded by woodland. When I look upwards, it's to the top of the trees where the branches are stretching, straining upwards – into what? What is the sky?

The Sky

What is the sky
But a backcloth for the trees
And the birds to fly through,
Cirrus dusted into speckled sprays
By the brush of the birch
Tinted by the larch
From the rays of the setting sun
And quietly, without fuss,
Painted grey, then black
By the cypress,
Before holding aside the curtain of the night
Showing planets and stars
In their orbital flight;
The sky is an illusion.

The Northerner

I longed for spring
After the winter gales,
And sleet and snow
And muddied feet;
And when it came, it
Quickly passed,
And summer followed;
And that was fleet.
Then autumn brought
Me thoughts of wind
And tangy air;
And, as a dream forgotten,
I awoke to the beauty of trees,
Stark and bare,
Of branches lashed with
Sleet and rain;
Of racing cloud and raging sea;
And my spirit rose and
Bid me greet the winter,
Which was part of me.

The Return

Like the eel to that strange and faraway sea,
Like the elephant to the last glade,
Like the wise man when he hears the call to
    go forth,
I, like them, have all my plans laid
To go north, to go north, to go north.

And why, and why, and why do I go?
To die? – Not to die. I say no!
But to a new life, which I hope to lead
Whether with joy or with strife
In that land where me ain folk breed;

Where the seas roar
And the long sands shimmer
And the hills march to the sky;
Where stand woods of oak and beech,
Where soft valleys lie, and wild misted moors
Stretch to horizons out of reach.
Where burns and rivulets
Flow to the Tyne.
Ah! that's it,
The reason, the Tyne.
The river,
My home,
Mine.

The Joy of the Country

A scene in Wales

The morning is still,
Mellow;
The stone walls are warm,
The sky is high and blue;
There is peace;
Even in the air there is peace:
The mountains enclose me in awe,
The river flows gently and sweet
. . . and then there comes the truck,
Packed tight with strangely silent,
Knowing-eyed sheep,
Bunched head to tail,
Fleece pressed tight.

The morning is no longer still,
Mellow;
Walls no longer warm;
There is lamb for lunch.

Understanding

Could we not be nurtured in some womb,
Lie there oblivious to growing,
No knowledge of birth, death or tomb,
No knowing, no knowing, no knowing
Until, and not until maturity,
With its power to cope,
Wakes us with enough light to see
The reason for pain, despair, love and hope.

Most days my one recreation is doing the Daily Telegraph *crossword. I've often thought it odd that, using my brain as I do, I no longer want to paint, or play the piano, or knit – I used to be a dab hand at sweaters – or do any of the things that are supposed to ease mental strain, but I do find great relief in using my bit of grey matter in solving the crossword.*

However, this morning, breaking off for a cup of coffee, I did not turn immediately to the back page of the Telegraph. *I glanced through the headlines, and when I had finished, even the crossword had no power to soothe me.*

Today

I can't bear the sorrows of the world:
The broken marriage,
The child dead through burns,
Going blind,
The torture of the prison camp,
Being found dead alone in old age,
Crimes committed, not in rage,
Cruelty to animals,
The experimenting in cages
For the good of humanity,
The things men do to their wives
Under the guise of love,
The pain of disease,
The frustration of the young,
The loveless life,
The hate between colours,
The ego and lust for power
Of the small man inside the big frame –
All is pain.

From My Bed

How beautiful you are;
How exquisite,
How divine.
You are single.
Unattached
And, what is more,
You are mine.

Your scent is beyond perfume,
It makes my senses reel;
Your touch is like velvet,
Your colour passionate;
Yet serene you stand in cool clear water,
Crystal supports your pose:
And this is how it should be
For the most perfect, perfect rose.

Silence

I listen to the silence,
For then memories have their sway:
Memories buried in the past,
Too weak to penetrate the day.
But in the silence
I hear them sharp and clear:
Memories of strife,
Struggle and fear,
Creating grief
Without relief.
Yet, in the silence
They are softened,
Muted with age,
And the silence tells me
Each memory was a page
Printed for my life,
A page I had to read,
Then act, to complete the play
That has brought me
To the chapter
In which I comprehend
That in silence was the beginning,
And in silence is the end.

PART TWO

THE DAILY ROUND

Slow Me Down

Why doesn't the earth too shrivel with age?
Why are the dawns still rosy with
    light spreading into day?
Why should I be loaned just one atom of life?
Why was I not endowed with
    spring-like seasons to renew my birth?
For are not my veins still full, my head sane
With urge and strife to go on living
    on this revolving plane?
What benefit can the gods hope to gain
From allotting me this meagre span?
If only in my youth I'd known of the
    shortness of life,
I would have walked my days
And never run.

Just a Saying

In childhood when the squabbles flare,
And to the origin of the fight
There's not a clue
Except the words
I'm not kind with you;

And in youth,
When first love's pain rips the breast,
Your best friend,
Who's without a lad,
Tells the world with joy
That stems from her jealous core,
She's not kind with him any more.

And in the middle of marriage
When hearts are sore
And the tie is about to snap,
They say of him:
Oh he's not kind with her,
She's played him dirty
And he's a decent chap.

But when in age,
And habit stales,
And conversation is rare,
They say no more,
She's not kind with him,

He's not kind with her;
Their lives,
Like the ebb tide, run over the sand;
Their time is running out.
What is left?
Only to be kind to him,
To be kind to her.

Youth

Youth is but a field of weeds and tares
That harvest the blind years;
And until they are scythed,
New seed will not rise.

I Am Young

I am young, I am tall,
I am young, I am small;
I am young, I am pretty,
I am young, I am plain;
I am young, I can walk,
I am young, I am lame;
I am young, I am well,
I am young, I am ill;
I am young, I am black,
I am young, I am white;
I am young, I can see,
I am young, I am blind;
Whichever one of these I am, dear Lord,
I pray you, keep me kind.

Laugh Gentle

Laugh gentle at the old,
Loud with a clown,
Chuckle at wit,
Bellyache at the comic,
Gurgle with a child,
Twinkle between friends;
Laugh at the world all you can,
And with, but never at,
Your man.

Washday 1912

Lace curtains, starched and dolly-tinted;
Thank God, last of the wash:
Moleskin trousers standing stiff with frost,
Soapy suds tipped from the tub into
    the backyard,
A broom wielded backwards and
    forwards hard,
Buckets of clean water skimming the dirty
    froth like a rushing tide.
Why does she complain about a pain in her side?

The Workers

Without work the days are long
And the nights are longer,
And the weeks stand still in frustrating ease,
Which slide into months of boredom,
And the year is gone without appease.

And in the days that are long
And the nights that are longer
Respect shrinks to a wizened core,
For work is the oil of man's existence,
And its wage, as had been proved before,
The only resistance
Against the endless death of enforced ease.

The Test

Written in 1925, aged nineteen

Sweet talk will butter us no parsnips
Nor fill the pot with taties.
When you find work we will wed;
Till then the fleas alone can share your bed.
So save your hands:
Whatever they arouse in me will stay
Prisoner in my womb
Until the day on the marriage bed
You sperm a child.
Legitimate . . .
No bastard on this straw.
So get you on your feet,
And do not hesitate
At the corner of the street,
But if you want me so sore
Find work
That will provide the taties and the rest,
And a bed
Whereon you can lay your head upon my breast,
And kiss me then fully on the lips.
But sweet talk will butter us no parsnips.

The Daily Round

Out of sleep I come,
Body soft-sweated,
Snuggled in hollow;
Protesting against day,
And standing straight
Dragging on clothes,
Fear of being late;
Her face from the gate,
When will you be back?

The train,
The factory floor,
The eleven o'clock sup,
The canteen,
The pub;
The train again,
Give your ticket up.

Home, she's at the sink.
What a day she's had;
Hasn't had time to think.
Tea,
Telly,
And to bed,
And sleep.

Would that I could sleep for ever,
Not too deep
But aware that I sleep,
Body soft-sweated,
Snuggled in hollow,
Nothing to follow,
Nothing to follow.

I have known so many women's lives spoiled with duty: the mother at seventy saying, 'Well, I won't be here to trouble you much longer,' and living on till ninety; a parent making a marriage almost unbearable, the wife torn between husband and parent. Yet when visiting an old people's home or hospital and seeing the hungry look in the eyes of those who have no visitors, I am apt to condemn the offspring who have abandoned them in their last years.

But there must be a happy medium, and I think the onus falls on the parent, for if they have acted with consideration and understanding from the beginning it would be a flinty son or daughter who would desert them at the end of the day.

The Dragging Chain

Beware the dragging chain of pity
That chafes your life,
Binding it with irritations,
Peevishness and lamentations
That for ever flick your conscience
With the singing whip of duty:
Compensation you must pay
For them having given you life,
And pretend gratitude
Which has gone for ever
With dead and unrequited love.

Beware the dragging chain of pity
That excuses domination
With filial claim,
Claim that sucks and leaves you
Spent and tinder dry;
No magnet in your turn
For chains to hang about your offspring
And claim their everlasting pity.

Tired

Tired: bones, flesh, brain
Battered with fatigue,
Soles hot,
Hands aching,
Back breaking,
Breath an effort
Butting against ribcage,
Eyes smarting,
Sweat parting
Hair into limp lanks of tow,
Shoulders heavy,
Legs protesting
Plead for bones, flesh and brain
A little resting.
But brain commands
One step more:
Do this, do that –
What,
In climbing a mountain?
No;
Just one more household chore.
Awaiting another fear to erupt.

Breakdown

I stand on the edge of the world
And dare not step further,
Stiff . . . frozen . . . paralysed
Before the void of eternity.
A small section in my brain
Says, move.
What! Into that?
NO! NO!
The world is revolving,
I will topple off.
No human hears my cry;
And God is not there
To hear my prayer.
My innards swirl,
Ordering my bowels to erupt
In disgusting spurts:
Step back!
Step back!
The toilet calls.
I am saved by nature's cry.
The void is covered
By a sward of green:
It is just the lawn;
The void
Is as if it had never been.
Comes respite, brief
Yet full of knowing,
Awaiting another fear to erupt.

I was looking at an episode of The Great War *on television that ended by showing a trench full of dead. I am usually horrified by these scenes, but on some of the faces there was a strange look, almost of peace.*

Death

The great peace
Lies on the faces
Of the dead.
Why should we mourn?
We who are left to fight life's agony
View not the torn limbs,
The burnt flesh,
We feel nothing but rest.
Let us envy their peace
And know that we too
Inevitably will experience their release.
Pray only that our end be swift,
For death has no terror,
The approach only is life's error.

New Epilogue

I have made the money,
I have won the race,
Prosperity greets me face to face:
Food in plenty, leisure in full,
Time to enjoy all wealth can cull.
Then why
Am I bereft of desire?
No urge to compete,
Imagination dormant
And memories lie still:
No groping to my beginnings
To enhance a tale.
My mind in stagnation lies,
Whimpering only that this is age,
A practice period before the final stage
Wherein might lie eternal peace.
But what if, there, a spiritual urge rears up
And greets me again face to face
And I am accused of dropping out
Before the race is run.
Will I be sent back to start again?
Oh, God, not another seventy-seven
        years of that!
All right, I'll stay and do the last lap.

Wants

Life is one long want:
From the womb to the tomb
The mind is taken up with wants:
Milk from the breast,
The grabbing for attention;
From crawling to sprawling in the form;
The rising want in the teens
When urges fog the mind
But make clear the kind
Of want the body craves;
The want cries loud when the wedding bells
      become a distant chime
And you change partners in midstream,
Only to find the boat so rocked
It washed away the cream
Of romance
Brought over from the wants of youth.
Life drifts on into age,
And still you want.
What?
Another man? Another woman?
Another friend? Death, the end?
Sadly the mind does not age with the body;
We want until the final breath.
If only we could learn to wait
Instead of want.

Loss

Happiness is the seedbed of pain
That generates sorrow.

I was happy in my love.
Tomorrow I knew must come
And tears would rain
And my heart would bleed.
If I had not craved happiness
I would have been inured
Against sorrow;
But life does not warn the heart
That from the joyish height
The fall is great;
And the seedling of love
Is now a sword,
And tomorrow has come.

Why did I not accept today?

Old Age

Old age is a blind
Behind which you are left with nothing
But your mind;
And this skitters,
Like an unruly child,
Dragging dead fragments from the past.
You scold it,
But without success,
For the child, as always, gets its way
So that peace can reign
In the house of the brain.
It is all childhood over again.

Night

Night is upon me.
I look through the pane,
And once again can see
The boy with the thorn in his foot.
The curtains are undrawn:
For I dread the hours ahead
And long for the morning
When, from this narrow bed, I shall
    greet the light
As it thrusts night into its place
That holds the dead and the dying
Of the human race.

Me

My left eye is going,
My right's not much good,
My blood is still spouting,
But that's understood;
My neuritis is a curse,
But the hiatus hernia is worse;
As for my allergy I scratch till I curse;
Then there is the spine,
Supported by arthritis,
And do not let us forget diverticulitis
     and fibrositis,
Nor the tic in the jaw,
Cystitis and bladder;
But all these are nothing:
What makes me madder
Is exhaustion, for it gets badder and badder
And leaves no room for anything worse,
And to be free from complaint
Really is a curse.
But goody-goody!
He's discovered a cyst
In an unmentionable place
I'm too refined to list.
The Gods are so good to those they love,
We have so much to be thankful for,
Heavens above!

I've been sitting still, quite still for two days and nights, in case I bleed again. If I can keep it up for another forty-eight hours I may beat it. It doesn't worry me half as much as the look on Tom's face; he hardly leaves me.

17 March 1970

Who suffers more?
I, with weakness shrinking my body,
Or my loved one,
Sitting wide-eyed, watching
Through the night.

The weakness is me;
And I am it,
Lost in a lone fight,
Grappling,
While my loved one is
A thousand beings:

Living our lives
A day at a time,
Pulsating years to space
And back into eternity
On old memories,
All fringed with fear,
While I am embraced
By myself alone,
And myself is weakness,
A ghost of her I once was.
Yet who suffers more?

Retirement

When I retire,
I said,
I'll read literature,
Great books of the past.
Time will be mine at last;
In it I'll delve
Into Pope, Milton and Voltaire;
Writings rare
Which will enrich my mind
And tongue
And allow me to talk
With authority
And earn respect.

I retired,
And with the promise to myself
I read.
At least I started,
Then parted
With Pope, Milton and Voltaire,
Again to stare
At the opiate
At which my mind had sucked
Tight pressed
To its breast
For twenty years.

Too late,
The pattern's already cut;
My mind,
Drugged by the one-eyed mother,
Laps the diluted
Turgid thought
Of those who did read
When I, abed,
With lazy mind,
Did not take a book,
But with pillowed head,
Eyelids drooping,
Slept,
Knowing that tomorrow
I'd be told
What I should think.

Anyway,
Why waste good telly time
To read,
Except a paperback,
With cover of naked skin
Which pleads
For your body's needs
And over which you can skim
To bits
That excite your flesh

And prepare you for the night
And the telly,
And flight
From reality and retirement.

So Easy to Read

They say that my books
Are so easy to read,
Simple.
They know nothing
Of the profundity of thought,
The depth at which they are wrought,
In the midnight sleep-seeking hours
Or in the breaking light of dawn;
And beyond it,
Dragged up and sieved
Through the grid of deletion
Until the clear essence,
In spare syllables, remains,
So those who run can read
And exclaim
In pain-filled breath of discovery,
That's exactly what they've always said,
At least that's what they meant
And would have said
. . . And written
Had they time to think it out.

But what matter?
It is their gain
If they can understand me;
My aim is accomplished
Through the crucible of pain.

Age

The dawn lifts the heavy-swaddled
    night to morn
And paints the hills with shots of red,
Foretelling the rain, wind and storms ahead.
Maybe it will be soft,
And its hue merely rose.
I lie in wait and ask
Which would I choose
Either. Either.
If once again I could tramp
The twisted path to the scree-covered slope . . .
Quiet. Quiet.
The time is past for hope;
Be satisfied
Waiting for the swaddled night
To lift to light.

Auto-suggestion

Through the strength of the eagle,
The mountain,
The sea,
This body of mine shall feel the power
To fly,
To leap,
To spring:
I will be king
Of health
And all it does hold fast
At last.

My spirit shall spurn decay
And, stooping low,
Drag my earthbound mind free
From weariness and despondency,
And, climbing with it,
Present it vital, fresh
And free, glowing,
Before the force that made it,
And as like meets like
The spark shall never dim:
I shall know the love of God
Because I am of him.

Atmosphere

The air in the house,
Your breath and mine,
Fills the atmosphere
Like rare old wine.
We sit, we talk, we walk,
We lie together,
And the air in this house
Folds us like clement weather.

The walls are impregnated
With our thoughts:
Ambitions, desires, conquests,
Success wrought;
The floors are boarded
With lost hopes
That know no rest,
But the air we breathe
Still bathes us with what is best –
At least
For us.

PART THREE

MY HEART IS YOU

Another Kind of Love

Blood is thicker than water,
It's true.
But it indicates you should love
Where you hate.
Don't strain to love your kin,
Put distance between,
And stay away
To prevent ulcers.
And don't question when
The stranger in the street
Tugs at your heart,
For here is your kin,
The kindred spirit puts out its hand,
And shakes,
And awakes love.
So do you meet your mate.
No blood tie here but someone closer
        than your skin.
So don't worry
When you cannot
Love
Your brother,
Or your mother.
Don't wilt, as if under a sin,
You didn't ask for them to be your kin.
So throw away your guilt;
Love is no sin.

To All Bairns

To all bairns
Who own no name,
And who, behind laughter-lighted face,
Hide the shame
Of sin,
Which benefited their joy
Not a trace.

To all bairns
Who carry the weight of guilt
Of censure and law,
Who reach the courts,
The borstals,
The homes;
Look not in them for flaw.

Nor yet in their mothers,
Who were bairns,
Nor in their nameless fathers,
Who were bairns,
Right down the ages to time's start;
But seek the flaw in good men,
Who make laws for bairns to keep;

And having looked,
And found,
Ask that this law

That breeds a stigma,
That reeks its stench on woman
And calls her offspring
Bastard,
Be changed.

Do not ask me how
The victim's vision is distorted,
For in her mind
She is still a bairn,
And the flyblow of a system.

Protect Me

Protect me. Protect me
From myself.
Don't let me love again:
No more rending of my heart,
No more placating,
No more pleading for passion spent;
I know it all:
My face is scarred,
My soul is marred,
I want no more pain.
In your mercy
Do not let me love again.

Do not let me love again.
Do not let me look upon his face,
And see there the desire that matches mine,
For I'll be beaten before the battle has begun.
Do not let me love again.

The Lonely One

The room is filled with noise:
Chatter, laughter, bursts of song;
I hunch my shoulders against the roar.
People are flooding in,
Pushing at each other at the door.
A Happy New Year.
A Happy New Year.
Here's to us!
Hello there! Why, hello there!
Faces I haven't seen since yesteryear.
They pass between me and the firelight.
Deprived of warmth, I shiver.
The hubbub fades;
The chatter, the laughter and burst of song
Seep into the silence and are gone.
But the silence remains;
I still have that,
And the single bed,
The table,
And the knick-knacks,
And the radio chat.

Once Known

John, James, Thomas, Sebastian who?
That's what they say
When, from the second-hand rack,
They pick up the books
Of men whose names once hallowed the air;
Whose words, in reverence, I bowed before;
And the sight,
On platform far,
Created in me a great stupefying silence,
As if in penance for some deficiency in myself.
Only twenty years, and they say
John, James, Thomas, Sebastian who?
What did *he* do?

and I keep reminding myself that they will say the same of Catherine Cookson.

So don't let us pay too much attention to ephemeral applause, Katie . . . but still, I liked it; and why not enjoy the fruit in season?

There was once excitement and an art in a man un-
dressing a woman; but where's the art in stripping off a
pair of tights?

Like everyone else he has already seen her breasts and
navel, and the second piece of bikini hardly hides the last
bastion. I'm sorry for the modern man in a way. I should
hate to be a fellow today.

Going Bust

How does a man run his fingers
Through her hair
Stiff with lacquer,
Surprising to the touch,
Or gaze into eyes
Dripping black streaks
Down her cheeks,
Or put his lips to petals
Of paint.
Well, he does all this;
But when her breasts
Come away in his hands
It's too much.

Bottle Blonde

She was a bottle blonde
But not blowsy;
Although her bust bid you good day
Before her legs made way
For her buttocks to sway.

Do Not Tempt Me

Do not tempt me to slay;
In thoughts and in dreams
Keep my mind at bay.
Do not tempt me to slay
With my tongue or my eye,
For by such weapons
I too shall die.

Let them say what they say,
My neighbour and my friend;
Day runs into day,
My world will some time end;
The hurt and the pains
For ever cannot stay;
Only do not tempt me to slay.

Do not tempt me to slay
With a derisive laugh
As I listen to my friends' fancies,
Their aspirations, their chaff;
The point of laughter
Can be a deadly ray;
Do not tempt me to slay
In any way.

As Our Kate used to say, 'Don't retaliate, lass, just wait. Every dog has his day.' And she would add with a sigh: 'But some bitches have two afternoons!'

Bitches

Bitches are not female dogs
Who, filled with young,
Bask in praises sung
Or, mongrel bred,
Are threatened with instant sleep,
But women with forked tongues
Who flick them in deadly darts
At friends manacled by convention
Or too stunned to rear and strike in turn
And who, like their canine companions,
Cower as from a boot
Into some far corner;

But unlike the dog
Time does not make them fawn
But yearn for confrontation
And devise an arrow
For the vulnerable spot
To give the cruel bitch
The works,
The lot.

But the particular bitch,
Wily as the wolverine,
Beams with such soft affection
That to let loose your arrow
Would break all convention;

So you slacken the tension of your bow
And lo!
With steady intent
The bitch rears
And you again are rent,
Left spent
Panting, gored.

If there's any moral in these lines, it is keep clear of bitches, but if you must in your daily round encounter them, learn to smile a quiet, superior smile, for there's nothing maddens a bitch more than a smile that can outdo her own in guile.

There are among the bitches those who smile too. These are the ones who do it while cutting your throat.

Hello, Kitty Dear!

Hello, Kitty dear!
How are you?

Is it true that you are writing?
How clever
To come all this way
From your background of drink
And fighting,
And, really, no education!
My dear, how you must have worked.
And, of course, to you all the glory.
But tell me,
Did you get
Some educated person
To edit for you
Your story?

This, in so many words, was actually said to me.

Who's to Blame Him

Who's to blame him
For falling as if from the sky,
With bricks and all –
You cannot blame the passer-by –
She only winked her painted eye at the fellow
And added a grin . . .
The combination made his head spin.

On Your Wedding Day

To be happy be kind:
Don't go to sleep
On cross words,
For overnight
They become swords.

Always share what you've got,
Little, much, or a lot;
And worries too.

And never forget to say,
At least once a day,
I love you.

*One day I got stuck in a crowd and for a moment I had
to stand aside, near a shop window, where two men were
talking, and I overheard a snatch of conversation.*

*'Oh, he admitted he was a bit of a lad. Really, he was
a good sort, but she, she was never no good.'*

*'No, no; you're right there: she was never no good. And
to up and leave him like that . . . Well!'*

*I shook my head. He was admired for his infidelity and
she was damned. Things don't alter much.*

Opinions

He picked the woman up;
Took her,
Left her,
Then went home to his wife to sup.

Monday, Wednesday, Friday the same.
Come Saturday in the club
His exploits
Were accorded acclaim.

By! he was a lad, was Fred:
The tales he told of women,
Especially of Nellie Crane, and bed.

Nellie's man went to sea.
She should be horsewhipped;
But then Nellie Crane was never no good,
Too free.

But what do you think of the latest?
Fred's wife has done a bunk.
Eeh! he's right low,
His spirits have sunk.
That's women all over, lad;
Women are bad.

Let's face the fact that a good percentage of 'second time arounds' turn out quite happily, but also let's accept that many of those who burn their bridges wish to God they hadn't, and most of these are men.

Partners

Don't light the match to burn the bridge
Whose flames you hope will smoke out your past
Before standing on the bank
And taking stock of its structure,
For, once burned,
Its ashes will smart your eyes into seeing,
And the rejuvenated youth
You hoped to recapture
Will wear the face
Of unacknowledged age,
And all the looking back,
All the self-recrimination,
All the pain won't forge the girders
To build that particular bridge again.

One day I was discussing marriage with a friend in his sixties. He said to me, 'The modern young parent is blamed for this, that and the other, and their own parents are held up against them as paragons of all the virtues, yet in my estimation parents have always had a lot to answer for. When I was young it was considered to be your duty to work all your teenage days to repay your parents for the trouble they had in bringing you into the world, and in my case, if I'd listened to my father, I'd never have got married because he painted marriage as something between slave labour and hell.'

A Wife?

What is a wife but a torment
To the skin;
What is a wife but a pain
To begin;
What is a wife but a dream
In dead of night;
What is a wife but every woman, except mine,
Within sight;
What is a wife but something
To work and sweat for;
What is a wife but a name on
A certificate of law.

All these things in youth
I saw through my father's eyes;
And more, more.

Sisters All

Behind the walls life seeps into the stone.
Sisters all, but alone,
Remember your vows,
Bow your knee,
Listen to the bell,
Flee those thoughts
Of home, man and child,
For therein lies hell.

Short-skirted, modern-hooded
Teachers, nurses, out in the throng,
Be not tempted by the lighted room:
Your bridegroom awaits
Behind the stone,
Sisters all but all alone.

The years of a woman
Die with the change.
What is left but a pious shell,
A supposed insurance
Against purgatory, damnation, hell.
Pray that God will remember
That your blood
Has dyed the stone.

Sisters all – but all alone.

But what is the secret of those who smile and emanate peace? Perhaps the answer is, all women don't need men; and all men don't need women. Christ is unsexed.

Every time I hear of a couple separating or being divorced I am saddened. Who can apportion blame? Who dares apportion blame? Marriage is a career full of exams; some of them are too difficult for us to pass.

But it must be very hard to stomach when a woman in her late middle years is left for a younger edition of herself: some men remain boys all their lives and as such their companions must always be girls.

Brushed Nylon

He left her for a piece
Half her age.
The paper said 'Decree nisi';
Nothing about the rage of rejection,
The lacerated feelings,
The humiliation
Shredding the last tendrils of pride;
Body huddled in the wide cold bed,
Not naked now
To please, to titillate,
But wrapped in brushed nylon for comfort,
Holding only sweat
Brewed by thoughts of wasted years
And rejection
That will drop to deeper depths yet.

The bed is the world:
Bare, barren, no affection in nylon.
The long night waits for the morrow
When they, in mock sorrow
And so glib, say
'You're free, dear,'
And on a laugh, 'Women's lib!'
Fools . . . fools,
Fools of females.

The Loser

On no great billows of emotion was my
    love wrought:
No undertow of passion pulled at my heart;
No fever erupted like a waterspout;
No despair mangled my mind like
    meeting currents from great seas;
You came to me softly,
Like a dawn wind heralding summer's day.
You then sank into the still waters of my being
Down to depths never before fathomed;
And there you lie for ever, inward
To my seeing heart and mind.
Your depths are my sky:
I have but to look into my being
And my world takes flight,
But only in the quietude of the night,
For, in the day, rising from the darkness
And the deep still waters of my dreams,
I return to my nature in the light above;
For I am a shy man who has never known love,
And what you've never had you cannot lose.
Yet I am a loser.

Distant Friends

Should I send *them* a Christmas card?
Should I? Should I? Should I?
A year has gone and not a word,
So why should I send them a Christmas card?

What have *they* ever done for *me*?
Not a thing, not a thing, not a thing.
They haven't even bothered to ring,
So why should I send *them* a Christmas card?

Do they ever ask us round?
Never! Never! Never!
And others have been, so I've heard,
So why should I send *them* a Christmas card?

Yet the thought will not pass:
Christ in reality, or in fable,
Bids me remember good will and the stable.
Oh, send them a Christmas card!

We talk about individuality and being oneself, but what is oneself?

The Individual

I'm not his or hers
Or theirs,
I'm mine
Me, self,
Whole
Individuality at its essence.
Why say you know me?
I don't know you,
Just what you care to tell.
Do you feel my pain, I yours?
Have you been down
To my particular hell?
Do you stir to my joys
Or struggle in the agony of my mind?
No, no.

Then why do I seek you out,
Need to be close to you
And all mankind?
Is it because I, and you,
And all are one,
No division:
Father, mother, sister, son,
Lover, neighbour, enemy, friend,
Black, white and yellow
Form the whole.
Is this the individual?

A Son

The seed bursts on what ground it falleth
And throws off with unthinking disregard
        its shell,
To suck from the black soil its sustenance
Until, gripping the light, it extracts
Its hue and in fresh-born colour
Pays to Earth its due,
Shining in harmony through its measured day
Until again claimed by the clay.

Not so a child,
Who struggles from the womb to light
And draws from the breast its sustenance to fight
The very breast that attempts to hold it;
For in thrusting it forth
The mother has not relinquished its mind,
And in holding mind
Has relinquished nothing;
Yet even mind, the powerhouse
Of all desire,
Has no power to hold
A son, once born.
Mother, if you want him to stay, let go.

Me Granny

Me granny sat in a wooden chair:
She had a stiff face, wrinkles and straight
    black hair;
But if ever I needed comfort I found it there.
Between her knees each day she'd have
    me stand,
And look me head for nits,
And I'd play the band until she said,
Here's a bullet! Mind you don't choke yourself,
It'll stick in your gullet.
Sometimes she sang her only song:
Love it is teasing,
Love it is pleasing,
Love is a pleasure when it is new,
But as it grows older and days grow colder
It fades away like the morning dew.
This song portrayed her life as a
    work-worn loveless wife.
She had a saying:
At my wedding I had no rice.
Me granny was nice.

The Virgin

In the depths of misery
I bewail my fate.
Is it too late?
Is it too late?
I'm one of the few, the rare,
Who have taken care
To keep clear of sin;
But the price to pay is high
To remain a virgin.
I haven't slept around,
I haven't had it off,
So why should they scoff?
And lay bets about my fall,
Impending they say as they giggle
And prophesy which lad will win.
The price is high to remain a virgin.

But there's one thing for it,
I found in my case:
I don't feel cheap and have to hide my face
When I forget the pill
And have to pay the bill
And be a single parent
Because he's on the run.

No, it mightn't be fun
Being a virgin in my single bed;
But it isn't all gloom,
For my mam and dad are sleeping
In their room, across the way,
And tomorrow is my seventeenth birthday.

What Is a Wife?

What is a wife but a caress
On my skin;
When she is not near
A pain within;
The reality of her body
In the depths of night,
And beyond other women
In the daylight;
A reason for working
And providing for;
The meaning of love,
And more, more.

That is how I saw my wife
In the heyday of my youth.

Forty years later

What is a wife
But a mate and a friend?
What is a wife
But a hand to hold at the end?
What is a wife
With eyes in wrinkles set,
But beautiful and soft
Even yet.
What is a wife

But memories to share?
What is a wife
But the reflection
Of my soul laid bare?
What is a wife
But God's promise of everlasting life.

Marriage – True Love

What has been one
Cannot be divided.
No cleft of death
Can take away
Those once loved:
The fingers once entwined
Will stay
Soft touched:
The lips that kissed
Will cling,
And bring
Memories like balm
And ease the heart
And dry the eyes
And whisper,
Sorrow, be gone!
What has been one
Is one.

Yesterday morning in the early dawn I watched Tom walking through the wood, trying to relieve a migraine.

My Heart Is You

Like Browning, I ask,
'How do I love thee?'
I love thee as I once did myself,
Asking happiness for me.
Now I ask it only for thee.
I ask it of the sun that goes down
And the pale morning light
That relieves me of my dream-ridden night;
I ask it of the dawn chorus that it may herald
    for you
A day free from pain;
I ask it of the rain
In which you joy to lift your face;
I ask it of the wind in the wood
Through which you walk
That it might blow through your head
And bring you back to bed
And me.

How do I love thee?
I cannot really tell,
For it is a pain
Like no known ache,
A pain with which I would not part,
For I treasure life,
And life is my heart,
And my heart is you.

INDEX

OF FIRST LINES

A bare patch of ground became a beautiful scene / 19

Behind the walls life seeps into the stone / 106

Beware the dragging chain of pity / 59

Bitches are not female dogs / 93

Blood is thicker than water / 81

Brittle leaves gold and brown / 24

Could we not be nurtured in some womb / 39

Do not tempt me to slay / 91

Don't light the match to burn the bridge / 103

From the seed all sorrow / 21

Happiness is the seedbed of pain / 66

He left her for a piece / 109

He picked the woman up / 101

Hello, Kitty dear! / 97

How beautiful you are / 42

How does a man run his fingers / 89

I am not blind / 13

I am young, I am tall / 51

I can't bear the sorrows of the world / 41

I have made the money / 64

I listen to the silence / 43

I longed for spring / 36

I stand on the edge of the world / 61

I'm not his or hers / 113

In childhood when the squabbles flare / 48

In the depths of misery / 116

John, James, Thomas, Sebastian who? / 86
Lace curtains, starched and dolly-tinted / 53
Laugh gentle at the old / 52
Life is one long want / 65
Like Browning, I ask / 122
Like the eel to that strange and faraway sea / 37
Look! I am alive / 17
Me granny sat in a wooden chair / 115
My left eye is going / 69
Night is upon me / 68
Old age is a blind / 67
On no great billows of emotion was my love wrought / 110
Out of sleep I come / 56
Protect me. Protect me / 84
Remember the summer of '69? / 22
She was a bottle blonde / 90
Should I send *them* a Christmas card? / 111
Sweet talk will butter us no parsnips / 55
The air in the house / 78
The dawn lifts the heavy-swaddled night to morn / 76
The great peace / 63
The meadow, sheep-cropped to earth's grey / 32
The morning is still / 38
The pall of Christmas hangs again / 26
The room is filled with noise / 85
The seed bursts on what ground it falleth / 114

The windows are clean / 29
They say that my books / 75
Through the strength of the eagle / 77
Tired: bones, flesh, brain / 60
To all bairns / 82
To be happy be kind / 99
What has been one / 120
What is a wife but a caress / 118
What is a wife but a torment / 105
What is the sky / 35
What rhymes with cat? / 30
When I die / 28
When I retire / 72
Who suffers more? / 71
Who's to blame him / 98
Why doesn't the earth too shrivel with age? / 47
Without winter, what would spring do? / 25
Without work the days are long / 54
Youth is but a field of weeds and tares / 50